Dear Dog

Anyone who has e̶v̶e̶r̶ ... want to live without one again. A dog is family member, watchman, protector, playfellow, and someone to talk to. A dog can be very important in the development of a child, and for an only child can be a substitute for the missing siblings. A child with a dog to look after learns responsibility and concern for others at an early age. On the other hand older people often seek comfort in an animal to help deal with loneliness. Of course dogs can't talk, but they are masters of an art that most humans never learn in a lifetime: the art of listening. Over the course of centuries, human beings have developed dog breeds for different purposes—they may be suited for hunting or for protection, or on the other hand may simply be loyal friends.

Barron's Mini Fact Finder *Dogs* introduces you to the best known and most popular breeds. The well-known dog photographer Monika Wegler has provided the expressive photographs of prize-winning pedigreed dogs. The comical puppies on the inside of the jacket and on pages 2 and 3 will enchant you and should be especially pleasing to children. The brief, easy-to-understand descriptions by Ulrich Klever, author of many popular dog books, give information about identifying markings and characteristics of the breeds depicted and offer tips on care.

The breeds are arranged by size and indicated by the colored code marks:

Very large and large dogs

Medium-sized dogs

Miniature and toy dogs

Pages 4 and 5 give you some "Interesting Facts About Dogs." There is a "Glossary of Terms" on pages 62 and 63.

With this handy pocket guide to dogs you can always identify unfamiliar breeds and can also learn something about them.

Puppies Between 6 & 8 Weeks Old

Collie

German shepherd

Irish setter

Longhaired dachshund

Yorkshire terrier

Bernese mountain dog

Beagle

Wirehaired dachshund

Cocker spaniel

Basset hound

Amazing Facts About Dogs

Breeds

Dogs are said to be the oldest domesticated animals. Some 12,000 years ago, when humans were nomadic hunters, they used dogs as their companions. Over the centuries people have developed countless breeds of dogs, each of which displays its own special characteristics. Today there are about 400 dog breeds, of which about 200 are registered by clubs and societies. Some breeds consist of only a few animals; others, such as the cocker spaniel or the German shepherd dog, have tens of thousands.

Large and small

Dog breeds can differ greatly from one another. Thus according to the *Guiness Book of Records*, a Great Dane in England is the largest dog in the world, with a shoulder height of 41 inches (105 cm), and a Yorkshire terrier with a shoulder height of 3½ inches (9 cm) holds the world record for smallness and is also the lightest dog, weighing nearly 10 ounces (283 g). The heaviest is a mastiff from the United States weighing 328 pounds (149 kg).

The Fastest

Dogs are fast runners. The fastest dogs are greyhounds and related breeds. The greyhound holds the speed record at 42 miles per hour (67 kmph). The saluki can run up to 34 miles per hour (55 kmph); the whippet, up to 32 miles per hour (52 kmph); and the borzoi can reach 31 miles per hour (50 kmph).

The Strongest

The heaviest load that a dog has ever moved is a railroad track weighing 7 tons (2905 kg). In 1978 the Saint Bernard Brandy Bear from Bothwell, Mississippi pulled one on a four-wheeled cart for 15 feet (4½ m) in less than 90 seconds.

Age

Tibetan terriers, with a life span of up to 20 years, are the Methuselahs of the dog breeds. Great Danes and bulldogs live an average of only 7 to 9 years. The happy medium is between 10 and 14 years. The oldest dog in the world, the sheepdog Bluey from Australia, lived to the age of 29 years and 5 months (died in 1939). The old formula that 1 dog year equals 7 human years is widely known, but it isn't quite accurate. At 12 months a dog is fully mature; therefore, 1 dog year equals about 14 human years, 2 dog years equal about 24 human years, and 6

Vocalization

There are noisy breeds and quiet ones. The ''talky'' breeds include the keeshond, German shepherd dog, and basset hound; the quiet ones include the chow chow and dalmatian. The vocalization ranges from whimpering and growling to barking and loud baying. Audible dog language can only be understood in conjunction with body language. A barking dog with a wagging tail means welcome, whereas a stiff tail warns you not to come any closer. A growling dog with bristling fur is signaling readiness to attack.

Running

Dogs are always in a hurry; as carnivorous hunters they had to chase down their meals. Their normal gait is the trot, hence dogs like to pull on the leash if our pace is too slow for them. Breeds like poodles and whippets have a prancing gait, the Old English sheepdog moves at a shuffle. All healthy dogs are able to run for extended periods; the record holders are the huskies, who not only can cover long distances but can also pull heavy loads while they are doing it.

Smell

Human beings live in a visual world, dogs in an olfactory one. Dogs ''see'' their environment through their nose. Tests show that dogs are able to detect specific scents at concentrations 1000 times lower than those detected by humans. Millions of scent cells, communicating with an enlarged, scent-specialized portion of the brain, perceive minute quantities of scent molecules, classify them, and store them in a scent memory. This enables dogs to find their way home, follow tracks, locate people buried alive, and search out poison gases or even explosives in sealed containers.

Hearing

Dogs bark even before a stranger rings the doorbell. They have a larger hearing range than humans and perceive sound frequencies beyond our range. Dogs point their ears to catch sound waves and can use 17 different muscles to move their ears. In dogs with erect ears one can see clearly that the ears are formed as funnels for trapping sound waves. But dogs can also close the inner ear so that it shuts out sound and thus consciously fail to hear. Dachshunds are masters at this!

Very Large and Large Dogs

Irish Wolfhound

Dog, cream-colored, 3½ years (r.); bitch, brindled, 3½ years (1.)

This gray giant is the largest dog in the world. Nobles used this dog to hunt wolves or to pull an opponent from his horse.

Appearance: Up to 35 in (90 cm) high, about 121 lb (55 kg) in weight. Muscular body, long head, formidable aspect. Rough, hard coat, especially long on lower jaw and above the eyes. Colored gray, brindle, red, black, pure white, fawn.

Character: Good-natured, patient, very devoted to its master, reserved with strangers.

Maintenance: Needs much space and exercise, long walks daily (off leash), or running next to a bicycle. Needs an even-tempered master who can train it consistently but without harshness.

Grooming: Brushing and combing daily, currycombing once or twice a week.

Remarks: Completely unsuitable for a pen. Must never be trained to become aggressive (may become dangerous).

Dog, fawn, 2 years

This dog is said to have been brought to Europe by Phoenician traders. Breeders call the Great Dane "the Apollo among dogs."

Appearance: At least 33 in (85 cm) high; weighs over 187 lb (85 kg). Noble, powerful body structure with expressive head. Short, thick, smooth, gleaming coat. Five colors: fawn, brindle, white and black harlequin, black, and blue.

Character: Self-confident, intelligent, quiet, not a fighter. Reliable watchdog. Good with children.

Maintenance: Needs plenty of room—if possible a house with a yard. Needs much movement and activity. Requires a consistent, firm but loving hand.

Grooming: No special problems.

Remarks: Because of its awe-inspiring size, many people fear the Great Dane. But the dog becomes aggressive only if its master is threatened.

Saint Bernard

Bitch, longhaired, 4 years

Because of its great size, the Saint Bernard was used at the beginning of the 19th century as the rescue dog of the Hospice of St. Bernard in the Swiss Alps. The most famous dog, Barry, is said to have saved the lives of 40 people.

Appearance: Up to 27½ in (70 cm) high, weighing about 176 lb (80 kg). Muscular body, massive head, majestic, commanding respect. In the long-haired variety, medium-length, sleek to slightly wavy coat; in the short-haired, short and thick. Both varieties white with red; feet, chest, and tip of tail always white.

Character: Quiet to phlegmatic, good-natured. Learns easily. Fearless, with fighting instinct. Good with children. Good watchdog.

Maintenance: Not a city or apartment dog. Can be kept outside, but needs a strong family bond.

Grooming: The short-haired varieties need little grooming; the long-haired ones need frequent brushing and combing.

Remarks: Some strains tend to be aggressive.

Dog, 5 years

The Bernese mountain dog is descended from the old Swiss farm dog breeds and is used —and superbly well suited— for herding and protecting cattle. **Appearance:** Up to 27½ in (70 cm) high, weighs up to 88 lb (40 kg). Powerful, massive. Soft, shining coat, sleek and long, slightly wavy. Black with light russet markings on legs, cheeks, and above the eyes; white head marking, white chest spot, often also white feet and tail tip. **Character:** Uncomplicated, with even temperament. Can, if necessary, grip fiercely without biting. Good, dependable watchdog. Affectionate and good with children. **Maintenance:** Needs plenty of space and exercise. When kept outside, needs to be fully integrated into the family. Easy to manage. **Grooming:** Regular, thorough brushing. **Remarks:** Should not change owners after age of 18 months. Can sometimes be stubborn or even aggressive with other family members.

Dog, 3 years

This herding dog comes from Hungary but has a Turkish name meaning "trusty guardian."

Appearance: Up to 29½ in (75 cm) high; weighs up to 88 lb (40 kg). Large, robust, and well proportioned. Coarse, wavy coat; some feathering on tail. Pure white or ivory.

Character: Very brave and intelligent. Does not submit easily, but follows its master; mistrustful of strangers. Devoted.

Maintenance: Not an apartment dog. Can be kept outdoors if close family contact is maintained. Needs a strong-willed master with experience in handling dogs.

Grooming: Must be brushed and curried regularly.

Remarks: Needs close human contact or will revert to wildness and become dangerous.

The first breed club for New-
foundlands was founded in
England in 1886. These dogs
helped Newfoundland fisher-
men to pull their nets to shore.
They are the best swimmers
among dogs.

Appearance: Up to 29½ in
(75 cm) high, weighs up to
150 lb (68 kg). Powerful and
strong, very thick fur. Webs
between toes. Long, smooth,
thick coat. Black or (rarely)
brown. The large black-and-
white *Landseer* is a separate
breed, recognized by the
Fédération Cynologique Inter-

Dog, black, 2 years (l.); dog,
brown, 6½ years (r.)

nationale (FCI) since 1960.

Character: Peaceful. Good
watchdog that barks little. Very
closely attached to humans.
Does not tolerate being in
strange hands. Strong protec-
tive instinct.

Maintenance: Not a city or
apartment dog. Except for its
love of water, this dog is not
demanding.

Grooming: Curry regularly;
do not bathe.

Remarks: Easily trained to
rescue drowning victims.

Dog, black, with red and brown markings, 6½ years

The German shepherd is the most popular working dog in the world and the best known of the dog breeds.

Appearance: Up to 25½ in (65 cm) high; weighs up to 77 lb (35 kg). Extended, muscular body; long or short hair; bushy tail. Black with yellow to light gray markings.

Character: Brave, but also sensitive. Eager to learn and to submit to a master. Well suited as a watchdog, guard dog, rescue dog, search dog, and Seeing Eye dog.

Maintenance: Can be kept in large apartments, but fares better in houses with yards; can also be kept in a pen. Needs a consistent hand, careful upbringing, and training.

Grooming: Thorough brushing daily, especially in shedding season.

Remarks: Dogs that are poorly trained bark and bite.

Boxer

Bitch (r.) with cropped ears; dog (l.) with uncropped ears

The first boxer resulted from a cross between the German bulldog and the Great Dane, which occurred in Munich in 1895.

Appearance: Up to 25 in (63 cm) high; weighs about 66 lb (30 kg). Square, sturdy, muscular body, grim facial expression. Short, shining coat. Red, yellow, and all intermediate tones; also brindled; frequently with white markings on head and/or chest; black face mask.

Character: Good-natured, high-spirited, and brave. Playful well into old age. Intelligent and, with consistent training, easily directed.

Maintenance: Needs a roomy apartment, regular exercise, and a daily play session. One should also work with this dog, which is one of the recognized working breeds.

Grooming: Care of coat offers no problems.

Doberman Pinscher

Dog, black, 2 years

This German dog breed was first developed in 1860; it is named after the tax collector Dobermann, who needed a fierce dog to protect him.

Appearance: Up to 27½ in (70 cm) high; weighs up to 57 lb (26 kg). Strong, muscular, elegant. Short, hard, thick coat. Black, blue, or dark brown with rust markings.

Character: Spirited, fearless. Affectionate and sensitive. Devoted to its family.

Maintenance: Ideally needs a house with a yard; can also be kept in a pen. Needs plenty of exercise and work, a consistent hand, and solid training.

Grooming: Not demanding.

Remarks: Without the strong hand of an experienced dog handler or sufficient exercise and activity, this dog's overwhelming energy can hardly be contained. The consequences are outbreaks of aggression, unruliness, and biting.

Rottweiler

Dog, 6 years

In the old imperial city of Rottweil this dog was kept by cattle traders and butchers for protection.

Appearance: Up to 27 in (68 cm) high; weighs about 110 lb (50 kg). Sturdy and rugged. Coarse, flat, short hair. Deep black with clearly defined mahogany markings.

Character: Even-tempered, robust, fearless, steady, and reliable. Good ability to learn; with appropriate training, can serve as guard dog or watchdog. Obedient and good with children.

Maintenance: Not an apartment dog; best kept in a pen. Should have close contact with the family. Needs plenty of exercise and work, preferably in the training field. Needs a strong, experienced hand.

Grooming: Needs little grooming.

Remarks: Buy only from accredited breeders. Beware of dogs with grave character flaws; they can be unpredictable, malicious, and have a tendency to bite.

Golden Retriever

Bitch, 6 years (r.), with puppy, 8 weeks (l.)

Russian circus dogs of the 19th century, which were said to have a golden coat, are among the ancestors of this dog.

Appearance: Up to 24½ in (62 cm) high; weighs up to 70½ lb (32 kg). Muscular; expressive dark eyes. Smooth outercoat with thick, water-repellent undercoat. Gold, cream, or wheat.

Character: Easily trainable; learns easily and willingly. Very affectionate and good with children. Friendly family dog.

Active, eager hunting dog who loves to swim.

Maintenance: Requires a large apartment, preferably a yard. Needs plenty of exercise, things to do, and affection.

Grooming: Must be combed thoroughly every day and well brushed. Carries dirt into the house, especially in bad weather, and sheds.

Remarks: Gets along well with other house pets.

Dog, yellow, 6 years

Sailors brought this dog to England from Newfoundland in the 19th century.

Appearance: Up to 24½ in (62 cm) high; weighs up to 68 lb (31 kg). Ruggedly and massively built. Short, firm coat without wave; water-repellent undercoat; tail covered with thick fur. Uniform color, yellow or black, without markings.

Character: Lively, peaceful, easily trained and eager to work, fearless, reliable, and steadfast. Very devoted and good with children.

Maintenance: Very adaptable. Needs plenty of exercise. Likes to work and should not be pampered. Especially enjoys fetching. Well suited for hunting expeditions.

Grooming: Regular brushing, otherwise needs little care.

Remarks: Labrador and golden retrievers are used to search for narcotics and are also trained as Seeing Eye dogs.

Dog, 1 year

The Old English sheepdog looks like something out of a Scottish legend—in short, an enchanting dog.

Appearance: About 22 in (56 cm) high; weighs up to 88 lb (40 kg). Gives the impression of being compact, though body shape and face can only be guessed at under the long, thick hair. Shaggy, matted coat without curls, with waterproof undercoat. Gray, mottled gray, and blue.

Character: Spirited, good-natured, adaptable, but also self-assured and independent. Intelligent and teachable. Very family conscious, good with children, and playful.

Maintenance: Needs plenty of space, abundant exercise, much attention, and love.

Grooming: Thorough brushing daily (for about 30 minutes). Not a dog for fussy housewives; the long, thick coat is a dirt carrier.

Remarks: Outstanding watchdog and herd dog who does not bark unnecessarily.

Bitch, yellow and white, 14 months (r.); dog, tri-color, 5 years (l.)

This Scottish sheepdog has become famous because of the television series "Lassie."

Appearance: Up to 24 in (61 cm) high, weighs up to 75 lb (34 kg). Long body with deep chest. Long, thick, rough coat; the smooth variety has a short coat. Bicolor (white and tan to mahogany or gray-brown), tricolor (black and white with russet or gray-brown), and blue merle.

Character: Friendly, intelligent, and sensitive. Learns easily and is obedient. Devoted, good with children. Mistrustful of strangers.

Maintenance: Needs a large apartment (preferably with a yard), extensive exercise, and activity.

Grooming: Sheds and carries dirt into the house in rainy weather. Should be combed and brushed daily for about 15 minutes.

Remarks: Not inclined to gain weight.

An ancient dog breed originating in Afghanistan. According to legend, Noah took Afghan hounds into the ark.

Dog, red with mask, 15 months (1.); dog, blue, 3 years (r.)

Appearance: Up to 27½ in (70 cm) high; weighs up to 66 lb (30 kg). Elegant and dignified; long head. Long, silky coat. White, black, gray-brown, and rust-red; also bicolored and tricolor.

Character: Intelligent and alert, sensitive and devoted. Reserved but is not hostile toward strangers.

Maintenance: Requires a large apartment or a house with a yard. Should have plenty of free exercise to satisfy compulsion to run. Needs a sympathetic but firm hand.

Grooming: Daily combing and brushing; in damp weather, thorough washing and drying.

Remarks: The Afghan's heritage as a hunting dog reasserts itself periodically. Therefore, it should always be kept on a leash outdoors. Can run as fast as 28 mph (45 kmph).

Bitch, 3 years

Setters have been the long-haired pointers of the British Isles for 200 years.

Appearance: Up to 26 in (66 cm) high; weighs up to 70 lb (32 kg). Slender, muscular, elegant. Thick, smooth, flat coat, partly short and partly longish, with feathery fringe on belly, brisket, and neck. Chestnut red color.

Character: Intelligent and independent. Depending on breeding may be emotionally stable or oversensitive. Very devoted and good with children. Moderately good watchdog.

Maintenance: Requires a large apartment, preferably a house with a yard. Needs plenty of exercise and attention. Versatile hunter (depending on training).

Grooming: Daily brushing. Daily care of ears is important. Sheds seasonally.

Remarks: Doesn't particularly like riding in cars.

Siberian Husky

Bitch, gray and white, 7 years

The world's most popular sled dog, of Siberian origin, came to Alaska in 1900.

Appearance: Up to 23 in (59 cm) high; weighs up to 60 lb (27 kg). Rugged; a wolf with brown or blue eyes. Medium-length, supple outercoat over soft undercoat. From pure white to black; usually black and white with gray.

Character: Strong-willed, persevering, and robust. Devoted, good with children, and sociable. Because of their strong urge to run, huskies are not suitable as companion dogs.

Maintenance: Needs relatively little room inside the house but much freedom of movement outdoors. Will pull things. Needs a strong leader to obey.

Grooming: Needs thorough combing with a steel comb during the shedding season.

Remarks: Since order of dominance is important for huskies, meetings with other dogs can lead to a battle for power.

Dog, red, 6 years

In their native China these dogs have a long past. English trading ships first brought them to Europe in the 19th century.

Appearance: At least 18 in (45.5 cm) high; weighs up to 55 lb (25 kg). Very compact, lionlike appearance, dignified gait. Blue-black tongue and lips. Luxuriant, thick coat. Solid black, red, blue, cinnamon, cream, or white.

Character: Strong-willed to the point of obstinacy. A one-person dog, it does not relate well to children and rejects strangers. Outstandingly good watchdog.

Maintenance: Requires at least a medium-sized apartment, but can also live outside. Does not need much exercise. Needs an understanding but consistently firm master.

Grooming: Thorough coat care daily. Sheds heavily.

Remarks: Unhappy when separated from its master.

Dog, 3 years

This "king of terriers" was used to hunt otters in the water and on land.

Appearance: Up to 24 in (61 cm) high; weighs 49½ lb (22.5 kg). Wiry, strong tail. Dense, rough outercoat with short, soft undercoat. Tan with black or mottled gray saddle.

Character: Intelligent; good learner. Lively and playful into old age. Best family dog; very good with children and good-natured, but not very compatible with other dogs or house pets. Good watchdog.

Maintenance: Needs a large apartment, preferably with yard, regular and abundant exercise, plenty of activity. With loving treatment this dog can accomplish just about anything.

Grooming: Must be trimmed every 8 to 12 weeks.

Remarks: One of the recognized service dog breeds. Also an excellent performer in obedience trials.

Dog, red with light mask, 7½ months

The Akita originated in Japan. A solid and substantial dog, it is the most imposing member of the world-wide Spitz family.

Appearance: Up to 28 in (71 cm); weighs up to 106 lb (48 kg). Robust and sturdy. The ring tail is typically carried high. Stiff coat with a soft, dense undercoat. Commonly red with a lighter mask or chestnut with darker mask, but all colors permitted.

Character: Affectionate and obedient toward its family. Quiet, even-tempered, courageous. Rather indifferent toward strangers. Watchful.

Maintenance: Takes a great deal of love and patience. Likes to work and be occupied.

Grooming: Not much needed.

Remarks: Cannot be forced to do anything. Not suitable for people who appreciate subordination in a dog.

Giant Schnauzer

Dog, black, 4 years

The giant schnauzer originated in the mountains of Bavaria and in early days used to accompany the nobles as a watchdog.

Appearance: About 23½ to 27½ in (60–70 cm) high; weighs about 88 lb (40 kg). Strong muzzle; prominent eyebrows and moustache. Rough-haired, hard, thick coat. Pure black or pepper and salt.

Character: Energetic but obedient. Sensitive, patient, and good with children. Playful into old age. Good watchdog.

Maintenance: Should have a large apartment or house with a yard but can also be kept outdoors. Needs plenty of exercise and activity, otherwise may become troublesome.

Grooming: Regular clipping and trimming.

Remarks: The giant schnauzer works as a police, customs, and Seeing Eye dog and is also used to sniff out narcotics and explosives. Training must be very firm, since these dogs mature slowly and are very playful.

Bitch, white, 3 years

Poodlelike dogs were depicted in art as early as the 13th century; later they were painted by artists such as Rembrandt and Goya.

Appearance: Up to 23 in (58 cm) high; weighs 48½ lb (22 kg). Square body with well-proportioned shape. Profuse, woolly, coarse and curly hair, with characteristic cut. Black, white, gray, brown, and silver.

Character: Easy to train, sociable, brave. Lovable and very devoted. Not interested in other dogs and concentrates entirely on its family. Good watchdog.

Maintenance: Needs a large apartment, possibly with a yard, regular exercise, and playtime. Cannot bear being alone. Needs to be occupied.

Grooming: Must have thorough brushing and combing three times a week. Depending on cut, must go regularly to dog groomer. Needs to have ear care and regular attention to teeth for tartar control.

Remarks: Poodles can easily be taught to do clever tricks.

Dog, 4½ years

In earlier times the dalmatian used to accompany horseback riders and coaches. Because of the dog's learning ability and "colorful" appearance, it also was used as a performing dog.

Appearance: Up to 24 in (61 cm) high; weighs up to 55 lb (25 kg). Muscular and well proportioned. Short, hard, dense, smooth, and glossy coat. Pure white with clearly defined and well-distributed black or brown spots.

Character: Easily trained; possesses an outstanding memory. Adaptable, uncomplicated, and cheerful. Devoted and good with children. Very clean. Good watchdog.

Maintenance: Requires a large apartment, preferably with a large yard. Needs plenty of exercise and attention, otherwise becomes melancholy. Needs an even-tempered master because the dog reflects its master's moods.

Grooming: Not much needed.

Remarks: Becomes overtly resentful if mistreated over a long period of time.

Rhodesian Ridgeback

Bitch (1.), dog (r.)

An old South African hunting and watchdog breed with a distinctive ridge, a stripe of hair down the back that grows in the opposite direction to the rest.

Appearance: Up to 27 in (69 cm); weighs up to 77 lb (35 kg). Muscular, powerful body. Short, thick, smooth, glossy coat. Light to reddish wheat color; may be white on chest and feet.

Character: Calm temperament, but can be fierce with human and animal predators. Very good watchdog with outstanding sense of danger. Not a dog for everyone. With patient and sympathetic training can become a very faithful, easygoing dog that loves children. Matures late and retains learning capability for a long time.

Maintenance: Needs a house with yard, plenty of exercise, and work if possible.

Grooming: Regular brushing.

Remarks: This ancient dog needs close bonding with its master.

Bitch, red with white (l.), bitch, golden brindle (r.)

In the 19th century this dog was bred exclusively for fighting bulls and other bullterriers.

Appearance: About 21 in (54 cm) high; weighs up to 61½ lb (28 kg). Muscular build; long, oval head. Short, smooth, and glossy coat. Pure white with head marking (monocle), brindled or red, dun or tricolor.

Character: Strong-willed to obstinate. Can distinguish large from small and strong from weak. Unconditionally submissive to its master. Outstanding family dog.

Maintenance: Can be kept in an apartment of at least medium size or in a fenced yard. Needs firm training and much love.

Grooming: Does not require special care.

Remarks: In inexperienced hands or with bad training the bullterrier can become a dangerous, unpredictable "weapon."

Bitch, fawn, 4 years

"Heart with fur" is what people call this herd dog in its native France. This breed was already in existence at the time of Charlemagne.

Appearance: Up to 27 in (68 cm) high; weighs up to 66 lb (30 kg). Muscular and well proportioned. Thick, long, shaggy fur. Black, gray, rust-brown.

Character: Intelligent, lively, spirited, and alert. Tough dog with a tender spirit. Loves its family above all. Hates to be alone. Good with children.

Maintenance: Not an apartment dog but also doesn't do especially well in a pen. Needs to be kept busy.

Grooming: Regular brushing and combing, occasional bathing. Loves rainy weather and brings dirt into the house.

Remarks: If not kept sufficiently occupied, it will find things to do, and that can often result in unpleasant surprises.

(1. to r.) **Dog, orange-roan, 5 years; bitch, brown-roan with tan, 4 years; dog, blue-roan, 4 years**

"The dog with the eyes that never lie" is a diligent hunting dog that has become a family and companion dog.

Appearance: Up to 16 in (41 cm) high; weighs up to 32 lb (14.5 kg). Strong and compact body; tail carried high. Smooth and silky coat, not wavy. Solid black or red, black with red markings, black and white, orange and white, black and white with tan, brownish gray, orange-gray with tan, and blue-gray.

Character: Playful, spirited, affectionate. Devoted and sensitive. Easy to guide.

Maintenance: Can live in a medium-sized apartment, preferably with a yard. Should have a long walk daily. Needs firm training; takes advantage of any weakness in the owner.

Grooming: Regular brushing and combing. Frequent ear examination and cleaning.

Remarks: Loves to eat and tends to get fat. Check weight often.

Bitch, 2½ years

This dog became very fashionable during the reign of King Charles II of England.

Appearance: Up to 12 in (30 cm) high; weighs up to 17½ lb (8 kg). Top of head flat; tail medium long, sometimes docked. Long, silky coat without curls, but can be wavy. Black and white with red markings; chestnut brown on pearl white background (*Blenheim*); blackish red or deep red (*Ruby*); black and tan (*King Charles*).

Character: Cheerful and lively, very friendly. Easy to train. Even-tempered, very trusting, and good with children. Gets along well with other dogs. Good companion dog.

Maintenance: Very adaptable. Can be kept in a small apartment, but with sufficient space it is possible to keep two or three dogs of this breed. Likes long walks.

Grooming: Daily brushing and combing.

Remarks: Requires regular checking of the ears and tear ducts of the eyes.

Dog, wirehaired, 2½ years

In the early 19th century fox terriers were used for fox hunts. The wirehaired terrier became highly fashionable in the 1920s and 1930s.

Appearance: Up to 15½ in (39.4 cm) tall; weighs about 17½ lb (8 kg). Dense, hard coat, kinky and wiry in wirehair, smooth and flat in smooth variety. White with reddish brown to black markings (wirehair); predominantly white with brown or black markings (smooth variety).

Character: Intelligent, steady, and daring; active but not restless. Needs firm training; tends to exploit owner's weaknesses. A cheerful dog.

Maintenance: Needs apartment of at least moderate size, with access to a yard if possible.

Grooming: Wirehairs must be trimmed four times a year. The smooth variety is easy to care for.

Remarks: Difficult to keep with other dogs, even of the same breed.

Dog, 2 years

This breed was developed in the middle of the last century when Scottish hunters wanted a white hunting dog so that it would not be mistaken for the prey.

Appearance: Up to 11 in (28 cm) high, weighs up to 22 lb (10 kg). Compact; short muzzle; short ears. Hard outercoat and thick, short, soft, nearly flat undercoat. Pure white without any shade of yellow.

Character: Very eager to learn. Robust; self-assured with other dogs. High-spirited with disarming charm. Good companion and children's dog. Good watchdog; not a yapper if properly trained.

Maintenance: Needs little space but sufficient exercise. Requires much affection but also firm training.

Grooming: Thorough brushing and combing daily; trimming every 3 months.

Remarks: Because of its ineradicable hunting instinct, must be kept on a leash in woods and fields.

The dachshund originated in Germany, where it is also called the *Dackel*. Because of its unique body shape, this dog was used by hunters to rummage through burrows of foxes and badgers.

Appearance: Standard-sized Dachshunds up to 10½ in (27 cm) high, weighing up to about 20 lb (9 kg). Miniature Dachshunds may weigh nearly 9 lb (4 kg) (dwarf) or almost 8 lb (3.5 kg) (rabbit), with corresponding height. Sturdy, short-legged, extended body with

Shorthaired: dogs, red, 9 years (1.), 4 months (r.)

head borne forward. Soft, silky coat, with tail carried like a flag; solid red or black and brown (long-haired strain). Wiry, thick coat interspersed with undercoat; beard and bushy eyebrows; all colors are admissible; white patches on chest, though allowable, are not desirable (wirehair). Short, thick, shining coat; solid red or black and brown (short-haired).

Character: A tough but lively dog, brave, intelligent, with a

high sense of self-esteem. Varying temperaments. Headstrong; can eventually develop into a family tyrant.

Maintenance: Apartment (size not important) should not be higher than 3rd floor or be reachable by an elevator. Needs to be kept busy and get plenty of exercise, but also enjoys rest. With a firm but loving hand the dachshund can be trained to be obedient and a hunting dog.

Grooming: Regular combing and brushing for the long-

Longhaired: bitch, 5 years (l.); wirehaired: dog, 8 years (r.)

haired strain. In general not much care needed. Wirehaired dachshund does not need trimming or clipping.

Remarks: Manipulating stairs, especially going down, is not good for the young dog. *Paralysis,* a blanket expression for slipped and ruptured disks that can befall these dogs because of their long backs, appears primarily at the age of 4 or 5 years and disappears forever after healing. Early treatment is crucial.

Dog, black and white (l.);
bitch, gold (r.)

A very lovable Tibetan breed. The word "apso" means covered all over with hair—a characteristic the Tibetan terrier shares with the Lhasa Apso.

Appearance: Up to 16 in (40 cm); weighs up to 31 lb (14 kg). Fine, long top coat; hair on forehead droops over the eyes. White; gold; sand; smoke gray; black; also two- and three-colored.

Character: Good watchdog; wary of strangers. Not a fighter, but will attack without hesitation if the occasion requires.

Maintenance: Needs regular but not very extensive walks.

Grooming: Time consuming: coat must be combed frequently. None of the hair should be trimmed.

Remarks: Must be trained early not to resist being combed and bathed.

Basenji

Descended from an ancient African breed that was never crossed with any other breed. The Basenji is also known as the Congo terrier or Congo bush hound.

Appearance: Up to about 17 in (43 cm) high; weighs up to 26½ lb (12 kg). Springy gait; small, pointed ears; deep wrinkles on forehead; tail curled over the back. Elastic skin; short, silky fur. Fox red, pure black, or black and tan. Feet, chest, and tip of tail always white.

Character: Very alert and

Bitch, red and white, 1½ years

highly intelligent. Socially gifted. Very devoted and serene. Obeys, though not unquestioningly. Very clever in getting its way, principally by charm.

Maintenance: Needs space and exercise. Happiest with one or two other dogs and will get along well with them.

Grooming: An ideal apartment dog; doesn't smell and is clean as a cat. Requires little care.

Remarks: This dog does not bark but yodels only to express great joy.

This unusually long dog can be stroked by three children at once.

Appearance: Up to nearly 15 in (38 cm) high; weighs up to 66 lb (30 kg). Low, sturdy, strong-boned and muscular body carried on powerful feet. Coat is smooth, short, and dense, not too fine. Usually tricolor—black, white and red-brown; also white with red-brown spots.

Character: Self-assured and determined, with a will of its own. Astonishing mixture of indolence and liveliness. Balanced

Bitches, tri-color

temperament. Basically friendly and easy to get along with.

Maintenance: Needs at least a medium-sized apartment and at least 1 hour of walking daily. Is hard to train; sometimes almost impossible to control on a leash; barks very loudly. Needs a strong and consistent hand.

Grooming: Not demanding but needs regular cleaning of eyes and ears.

Remarks: One of the best trackers; persists like no other dog.

Beagle

Dog, tri-color, 3 years

Descended from old English hounds, the beagle is the traditional dog for hunting hares either in a pack or alone.

Appearance: Not over 16 in (41 cm) high; weighs up to 39½ lb (18 kg). Sturdy and yet elegant. Short, dense, sturdy coat, usually in three colors. Tail is thick and densely furred, always with a white tip.

Character: Self-assured and independent; obeys only reluctantly. Sociable (especially enjoys company of other dogs) and devoted; the best with children. Does not feel attached to one person.

Maintenance: Adaptable. Regular walks, if possible running alongside a bicycle; always on a long leash. Not easy to train. Not a good watchdog.

Grooming: Not demanding.

Remarks: If allowed to escape their master's control, beagles are inclined to rummage or wander about. Many beagles get run over this way.

Dog, dark brindle, 3 years

Bulldogs were famed and notorious fighters of bulls, bears, and badgers. Some of them were as famous as today's football stars.

Appearance: About 15½ in (40 cm) high; ideal weight 53 lb (24 kg). Compact, broad, with a powerful skull. Thick, short, smooth coat. White, reddish, reddish yellow, fawn, or brindle.

Character: Self-assured, dignified, and reserved. Good-natured, trustworthy, and loyal. Shows more interest in its family than in other dogs; likes children.

Maintenance: Can be kept in a small apartment. Should have daily outings but not excessive exercise. Needs a great deal of attention. Can become obedient with loving, patient, and firm training.

Grooming: Regular and careful cleaning of the skinfolds.

French Bulldog

Bitch, spotted, 3 years

This French companion dog was created around 1880 by crossing bulldogs with terriers and pugs.

Appearance: Up to 12 in (30 cm) high; weighs up to 26½ lb (12 kg). Built square and strong; upright bat ears. Short, dense, shining coat. Pure white, brownish gray to black spots on white, various mixtures of black and reddish brown brindle, with and without white spots.

Character: Brave, active, and alert. Doesn't care much for submission but compensates by being very perceptive; understands every mood. Cheerful and amusing, though not without dignity. Very devoted. A fearless watchdog that does not bark without reason.

Maintenance: Can be comfortable in a small apartment and adapt to any way of life. Needs regular exercise. Needs plenty of love.

Grooming: Not demanding.

Remarks: The dog is a passionate rat catcher.

Keeshond

Bitch, 2 years

The favorite dog of the Dutch, the keeshond has long served as a barge dog on the Netherlands' many water ways. Today, it is also popular as a pet and watchdog—both in its native land and elsewhere as well.

Appearance: Up to 18 in (46 cm) high, weighing up to 40 lb (18 kg). Straight rump with a short back. Upstanding coat, particularly the mane, neither wavy nor shaggy; silver-gray with black shadings on nose, ears; legs and tail lighter.

Character: Very intelligent and eager to learn, good to lead. Devoted and loyal, loving with his own family. Dependable companion dog.

Maintenance: Large apartment, preferably a house with a yard. Needs much activity and something to watch over.

Grooming: Careful brushing daily, with a natural-bristle brush, from back to front.

Remarks: A friendly and affectionate dog that loves to be kept busy.

Of Chinese origin, the pug was introduced to Europe in the 16th century and evolved to its modern appearance in England.

Appearance: Up to 12½ in (32 cm) high; weighs up to 17½ lb (8 kg). Sturdy, squat, and muscular; deeply wrinkled forehead; double-ringed tail carried over the back. Short, glossy coat. Silver gray to apricot with black mask and dorsall stripe.

Character: Highly intelligent. Calm, cheerful manner; agree-

Bitch, stone gray, 4 years

able and lovable. Loves to play with children and is very devoted.

Maintenance: Can live in a small apartment. Needs little exercise but a great deal of loving attention.

Grooming: Daily brushing and regular cleaning of skin folds.

Remarks: Can become phlegmatic if not sufficiently occupied. Cannot stand any stress. Breathing is highly audible.

Bitch, yellow and white, 8 months (l.); dog, tri-color, 6 years (r.)

This herding dog from the Shetland islands has been called a "miniature collie," but actually it is a separate breed.

Appearance: Up to 14½ in (36.8 cm) high; weighs up to 39½ lb (18 kg). Body build like a collie's, but smaller. Long, straight, rough outercoat with furlike undercoat. Tricolor— black, tan, and white; red, black, and white; also blue-black.

Character: Learns easily and performs well. Alert and watchful; mistrustful of strangers. Adapts to the moods of its family.

Maintenance: Can be kept in a small apartment. Needs plenty of regular exercise and to be kept busy.

Grooming: Daily brushing and combing for 10 minutes.

Remarks: Although now a popular companion dog, the shelty is an outstanding herder of large sheep herds.

The standard schnauzer is the oldest member of the schnauzer family. The miniature is said to have been bred from the standard, the affen pincher, and the poodle.

Appearance: *Miniature schnauzer:* up to 14 in (35½ cm) high; weighs up to 15 lb (7 kg). *Standard schnauzer:* up to 19½ in (50 cm) high; weighs up to 40 lb (18 kg). Squarish but still elegant; wiry. Eyebrows and mustache define the face. Rough-haired, hard, and thick coat. Solid black or pepper and salt.

Character: Loves to work. Good-natured; playful into old

Standard bitch, pepper and salt, 6 years

age. Devoted and good with children. Outstanding sense of ownership makes it an incorruptible watchdog.

Maintenance: Comfortable in a small city apartment but needs to be taken out and exercised often.

Grooming: Trimming every 3–4 months; brushing of body, combing of mustache and eye brows.

Remarks: Excellent hunter of rats and mice. In the old days they were used to keep stables free of vermin.

This tiny dog is named after a Mexican city at the foot of the Sierra Madre.

Appearance: Never more than 8 in (20 cm) high; weighs between 17½ oz (500 g) and 5½ lb (2.5 kg). Round head with pointed muzzle; large bat ears. Short and dense or long and soft, glossy coat. White, chestnut brown, fawn, sand, and steel blue to black; also marked or splashed.

Character: Highly intelligent and lively. Very hardy, brave, and fearless. Not a dog for

Dog, apricot with white, 6 years (l.); dog, black and tan, 6 years (r.)

children.

Maintenance: Adapts to its owner, on whose arm it feels happiest. Loves activity; needs regular exercise and occupation.

Grooming: Long-haired strain needs regular brushing. Keep eyes clean.

Remarks: Although a ''lapdog,'' this dog pines when kept constantly in the house.

Dog, light red brindle, 1 year

Descended from dogs of the imperial palace of China, this breed was brought to Europe in the 19th century.

Appearance: Up to 10 in (25 cm) high; weighs up to 13 lb (6 kg). Body close to the ground, strong-boned. Double coat with thick underlayer and long, straight outercoat; has a mane. All colors.

Character: Self-assured and fearless. A daredevil with a strong will of its own. Needs a great deal of affection. Usually devoted to one person whom it does not want to share with anyone.

Maintenance: Likes a small apartment. Needs much attention. Should not be spoiled but firmly trained.

Grooming: Frequent combing and brushing; regular cleaning of facial wrinkles.

Remarks: Because of its loyalty and constant readiness to protect its master, this dog can become a jealous tyrant.

Shih Tzu

This Chinese dog originally came from Tibet; its name means "lion."

Appearance: Up to 10½ in (27 cm) high; weighs up to 15½ lb (7 kg). Long, dense coat with undercoat; tail curled over the back; beard and mustache. All colors, frequently with white spots on the face and a white tail tip.

Character: Very hardy and as robust as a working dog. Lovable and playful; good with children. Watchful, alert.

Maintenance: Doesn't need

Bitch, gold and white, 1½ years (r.); dog, gray and white, 3 years (1.)

much space but should have regular, moderate exercise and sufficient occupation. Binds closely to one person.

Grooming: Thorough daily coat care (brings much dirt into the house) with combing, brushing, and currying.

Remarks: It is practical to pin the "lion's mane" up on the head with a barrette or bow (especially before meals).

This dog, bred in the cloisters of the Tibetan capital of Lhasa, was produced by a cross between a terrier and a Tibetan spaniel.

Bitch, light gold, 1 year (l.), bitch, red-gold, 2 years (r.)

Appearance: Up to 10 in (25 cm) high; weighs up to 15½ lb (7 kg). Heavy, dense, abundant coat in 2 layers; neck with thick mane; fringed tail curled over back. Honey, sand, rust, and smoke.

Character: Self-assured, cheerful. Is usually attached to one person with great devotion and reacts to strangers with rejection and mistrust.

Maintenance: Doesn't need much space but needs a regular, moderate exercise. Requires much attention.

Grooming: Thorough combing daily; currying and brushing as necessary.

Remarks: The Lhasa apso is not really a dog for children, but it is an excellent companion for older people.

Bitch, 3 years (l.), and puppy 4 months (r.)

This terrier was bred in the 19th century in Yorkshire as a hunting dog (for entry into badger and fox burrows).

Appearance: Up to 9½ in (24 cm) high, weighs up to 7 lb (3.2 kg). Dainty, compact, well proportioned. Long, silky coat, hanging down on the sides. Dark steel blue from base of skull to base of tail; tan head, chest, and legs.

Character: Lively, self-assured, alert toy dog. Very devoted and playful. Sensitive. Needs firm training, otherwise tends to yap.

Maintenance: Suited for small apartments. Needs little but regular exercise.

Grooming: Daily brushing, combing, and light oiling; bathing once a month. The long hair on the head should be pinned back with a barrette.

Remarks: A fashionable dog, the Yorkshire terrier has been produced indiscriminately and is often overpriced. Buy only from a breeder.

Dog, orange, 1 year

The Pomeranian was Queen Victoria's favorite dog; in the 1920s it was the fashionable dog of France.

Appearance: Up to 8½ in (22 cm) high; weighs up to 6½ lb (3 kg). Straight body with a short back. Coat like that of the keeshond (page 48). Black, white, brown, and orange; also blue and cream, occasionally spotted.

Character: Like the keeshond but also cheerful and amusing.

Maintenance: Can live in a small apartment but should be trained not to bark at every sound.

Grooming: Daily brushing; also currying against the grain. Watch for secretions in the corners of the eyes.

Remarks: Has a piercingly high bark. Can be trained relatively easily to bark at the sound of the telephone or doorbell. This can be a great help to someone who is hard of hearing.

Standard bitch, black (l.); toy bitch, apricot (r.)

In the 19th century the writer Peter Scheitlein described these lovable dogs as follows: "The poodle is the most perfect dog. It has individuality, distinctiveness, originality, and geniality."

Appearance: *Miniature poodle:* up to 15 in (38 cm) high; weighs about 33 lb (15 kg). *Toy poodle:* up to 10 in (25½ cm) high; weighs about 9 lb (4 kg). Coat and coloring like the *standard poodle* (page 29); toy poodles can also be apricot.

Character: Like standard poodle.

Maintenance: Like standard poodle.

Grooming: Like standard poodle.

Note: Poodles must be clipped regularly. Recognized cuts are: *continental clip,* in which the jaw, hindquarters, and legs are clipped short, with cuffs on the front and back legs, pompom on the tail, and a mane on the head and chest; *sporting clip,* with trousers on the front and back body, a pompom on the tail, and long hair on the head and ears.

A very spirited toy dog that is a "big" dog in pocket size, the miniature pinscher is surprisingly robust in spite of its fragile appearance.

Appearance: 11 to 11½ in (28–29 cm); weighs 7–9 lb (3–4 kg). A miniature version of the Doberman Pinscher with a short, shiny coat. May be solid red or brown in various shades; two-colored with red or brown markings on black.

Character: Lively; very intuitive; affectionate; enjoys playing little tricks; totally devoted

Bitch, red, 2 years; bitch, black and red, 2½ years

to its people.

Maintenance: Likes going for walks. Doesn't mind being left alone occasionally.

Grooming: Not much needed.

Remarks: Dogs that have been bred smaller than the prescribed standard lose their endearing qualities.

Glossary

Banner: The long hairs on the underside of the tail.

Bat ears: Long erect ears, broad based with rounded tips.

Blue merle: Blue and gray marbled with black.

Brindled: Stripes formed by darker hair on lighter coat.

Color strains: Different coat colors in the same breed.

Cropping: Trimming the ears of a whelp.

Culotte (also **trousering**); the long, soft hair on the back side of the thigh.

Dewlap: Loose skin beneath the throat. Permitted in breeds like the basset hound.

Docking: Trimming the tail to suit the standard of the breed.

Double coat: Fur coat that consists of thick undercoat with medium-length outercoat, as in the German shepherd dog.

Eel stripe: A dark stripe running down the back.

Feathering: A fringe of longer, soft hair on the backside of the legs, ears, or tail.

Flews: The loose lateral parts of the upper lip. They are termed *pendulous* if they hang down, as in boxers, or *well filled* if they lie close, as in bullterriers.

Forequarters: The anterior (front) part of the dog including chest, shoulders, and front legs.

Fringe: The long hairs on the ear, as in the cocker spaniel.

Guard hair: Longer hair hiding a shorter undercoat.

Hindquarters: The posterior (back) end of the dog from the hipbone to the hind feet.

Long-haired: Used for dogs with an outercoat of long, soft hair — with an undercoat, as in the Newfoundland or without, as in setters. If the undercoat is thick and the hair of the outercoat sticks out straight, we speak of a long double coat, as in the keeshond.

Markings: Patches of brown, gray, black, or other colors (can also be flecked or marbled pattern) on head or body.

Mask: Field of color on the dog's face that is sharply delineated from the main color.

Muzzle: The front of the face, including nose and jaws.

Overbreeding: Intensive breeding for particular characteristics such as size, single body parts, or general appearance. This can result in physical or mental defects.

Pepper and salt: Dark guard hair with light tips.

Ringtail: A curled tail carried over the back or sideways, as in the pug and keeshond.

Rough hair: Short or medium-long guard har that is hard and rough to the touch and grows in different directions.

Rudder: A dog's tail.

Shaggy hair: Very long, coarse hair, as in the Old English sheepdog.

Short-haired (also **smooth-haired**): Dogs with an outercoat of very short hair over a thin undercoat.

Undercoat: Wooly hair beneath the guard hair; protects against the cold in winter and against the sun in summer.

Whelp: A puppy from the time of birth until all its milk teeth have grown in.

Wirehair: A coat of rough, short or medium-long hairs that feel wiry to the touch and stick out in all directions. Wirehaired dachshunds and various terriers are examples.

Dogs Index

English translation © Copyright 1990
by Barron's Educational Series, Inc.

© Copyright 1989 by Gräfe and Unzer
GmbH, Munich, West Germany
The title of the German book is *Hunde*

Translated from the German by Elizabeth D. Crawford
Consulting Editor: Matthew M. Vriends, Ph.D.
Photographer: Monika Wegler

All inquiries should be addressed to:
Barron's Educational Series, Inc.
250 Wireless Boulevard
Hauppauge, NY 11788

Library of Congress Catalog Card No. 90-35472

International Standard Book No. 0-8120-4457-6

Library of Congress Cataloging-in-Publication Data

Klever, Ulrich,
    [Hunde. English]
    Dogs: with colored photos of puppies to fall in love with:
  introducing the most popular dog breeds in the world, with tips on
  care / Ulrich Klever.
      p.   cm.
    Translation of: Hunde.
    ISBN 0-8120-4457-6
    1. Dog breeds.   2. Dogs.   3. Dog breeds—Pictorial works.
  4. Dogs—Pictorial works.   I. Title.
SF426.K5313   1990
636.7—dc20   90-35472
                                                        CIP

PRINTED IN HONG KONG

0123 9927 9876543